THE GOOD,
THE PLAID,
AND THE BOGEY

A GLOSSARY OF GOLFING TERMS

Illustrated by: Kevin Ahern

ALLIGATOR: A slimy, toothy creature frequently seen on the golf course. Not to be confused with a club pro.

AMATEUR: An honest scorekeeper.

BACKSWING: How to prepare your club for ball contact. A good one can insure victory, especially if you happen to catch your opponent's head with a 3-wood.

BALL RETRIEVER: 1) A long- handled device used to retrieve golf balls from the water. 2) An office underling trying to get in good with the boss.

BALL WASHER: See lake.

BIRDIE: 1) One stroke under par. 2) What you flip to the slow group in front of you who won't let you play through.

BRIDGE: 1) A small wooden structure connecting land over a water hazard. 2) That thing you almost swallowed on your last missed putt.

BUCKET OF BALLS: 1) What you drive on a practice range. 2) What you'll lose this season if you don't work out that hook.

CHIP SHOT: A golf swing popularized by a cast member of "My Three Sons."

CLUB: A thin metal pole used to test your throwing ability and knee strength.

9

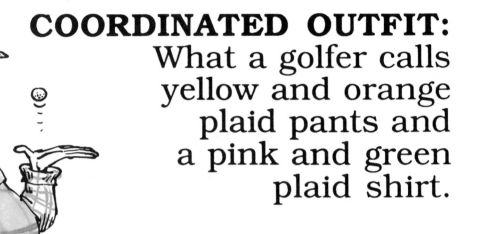

COORDINATED OUTFIT:
What a golfer calls
yellow and orange
plaid pants and
a pink and green
plaid shirt.

10

DIMPLES: 1) Indentations on the ball that make it fly farther.
2) Indentations on your backside after an errant drive ricochets off two saplings and a ball washer.

11

DOG-LEG: The shape of your club after you muff a three-foot putt.

DUCK: 1) A handsome waterfowl that makes its home on a water hole. 2) The traditional way to announce that it's your turn to tee off.

EASY PUTT: A putt made by another golfer.

ELECTRIC CART: A small motorized snack wagon.

15

EXERCISE: The main reason to golf, occurring when clubs are lifted from the trunk and placed onto the cart.

FAIRWAY: The rare method of playing that guarantees you'll never break 100.

FANATIC: 1) A person who is interested in a particular subject to an extreme degree. 2) A golfer.

FAST GREEN: What a golf hustler expects when he sees your swing.

FLAG: 1) A small triangle indicating the hole you're approaching. 2) A great big rectangle with a circle on it that indicates you've got a really bad slice.

FORE: What you swear you shot on a par five.

FOURSOME: Four guys playing together, each of whom thinks he's the best golfer in the world.

19

"GO IN! GO IN!": A phrase yelled by golfers attempting to sink a difficult putt, or by those playing behind a slow foursome.

GOLF: A series of difficult physical maneuvers, mental calculations and challenging decisions that after years of practice, dedication and sacrifice, will give you countless sunny weekends filled with frustration and humiliation.

GOLF BALL: A little white spherical object, often referred to in the air as "Oh hell."

GOLF TOWEL: A piece of absorbent cloth, covered with stupid sayings, which you are forced to use because it was a gift.

GRIP: The placement of hands that insures a successful game, depending on how tightly they are placed around your opponent's neck.

HACKER: Anybody who beats you. See "LUCKY JERK."

HANDICAP: A golf cap with a bottle opener attachment.

"HECK," "DARN" and "SHUCKS": Expletives that have never been heard on a golf course.

INTIMIDATION: A way to lower your opponent's score by mumbling things like, "Boy, I hope I don't lose and get so mad I do something that lands me back in prison."

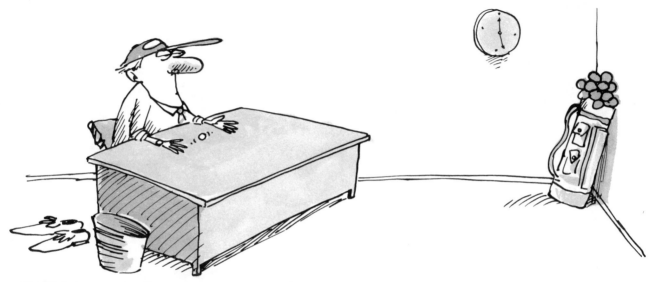

JOB: The stupid incidental thing you do between golf games.

KIPPER: Not really a golf term, but doesn't it sound like it should be?

LOSER: Anyone who gets stuck golfing with their spouse.

27

MASHIE NIBLICK: What happens when someone hits your niblick with a five-iron.

MULLIGAN: The god of misfortune who, if you call out his name enough times, can help you break 90.

NOVICE: A golfer who does not yet swear.

OPEN: An annual tournament where golf fans pay big money to sweat like pigs and watch professionals through cheap cardboard periscopes.

"OUCH!": The sound directly
following "Fore!"

OUT OF BOUNDS: 1) Refers to a ball that has left the field of play. 2)Unsportsmanlike behavior, such as questioning the honesty of others in your foursome, breaking a player's concentration with constant chatter, or sticking pins in voodoo dolls of other golfers during their backswings.

PAR: See "HOLY GRAIL."

PEBBLE BEACH: The course next to Bam Bam Beach.

34

PITCH AND RUN: The result of being paired up with an insurance salesman.

"PLAY THROUGH?": Requesting that the slower group in front of you watch you make the most dreadful shot of your life.

PRACTICE SWING: See "Whiff."

PRO-CIRCUIT: A bunch of spoiled wimps who've never worked a single day in their lives.

"PULL THE PIN": An expression used prior to blowing up your clubs.

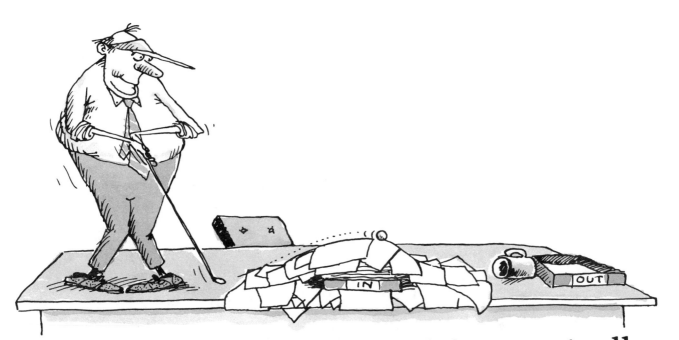

PUTTING PRACTICE: What typically goes on behind office doors when you're "in conference" all morning.

QUEASY: What other golfers get when they see you in shorts.

QUIZZICAL: An adjective used to describe the looks you get from your companions when you say the simple words, "Turkish rules today?"

41

ROUGH: Getting out of the house to play when there are chores to be done.

RULES OF GOLF: Official regulations that you should be familiar with so you can bend, twist, alter and reinterpret them to your advantage.

ACCORDING TO RULE 710-835.4D: THIS IS A "GIMMEE" WITH A PRACTICE PUTT OPTION...

"RUNNING IT ON THE GREEN":
Poor golf cart etiquette.

45

SAND: 1) What makes up two-thirds of the world's beaches. 2) What makes up two-thirds of your golf game.

SANDBAG: 1) To inflate your score to achieve a higher handicap. 2) What your body looks like after a summer of hot dogs, beer, and riding around in an electric cart.

SKINS GAME: A wager where you bet on one of two things-- either who will score the lowest on a given hole or who will blister the worst in the blazing sun.

SLICE: A serving of pie. That's all. Nothing else. Certainly not a fatal flaw in <u>my</u> game! No sir!

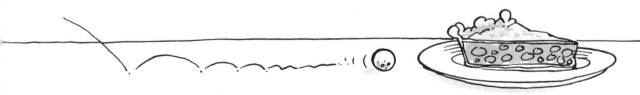

SMILE: 1) A savage cut in a badly hit golf ball. 2) The expression on your face when you say "Aw...too bad" after your opponent hooks his shot into the lake.

SPIKES: What a novice golfer does to his ball after he sinks a putt.

"STEP ON IT": 1) An expression used to encourage faster play. 2) What to do if you find your opponent's ball in the rough.

TEE: A little piece of wood that, with the proper swing, you can send flying two or three yards while it's still stuck in what has become a nice divot.

54

TEE TIME: A time on a sheet of paper that's 40 - 60 minutes earlier than when you actually tee off.

TIPPING THE CADDY: 1) Rewarding a helpful assistant. 2) What you do to the car of the rich guy who just beat you.

TWENTY FOOT: A standard measurement used to describe any putt you make.

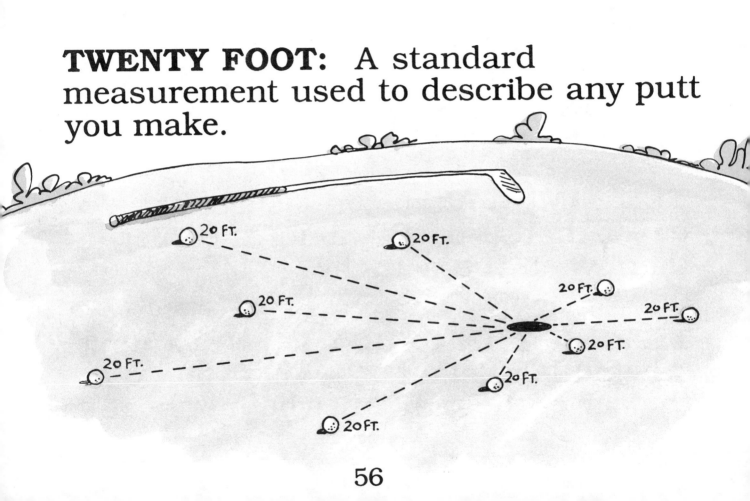

UMBRELLA: A collapsible device carried all over the golf course on sunny days, and left at home when it rains.

UPHILL LIE: The act of writing down your score while walking uphill.

V-SIGN: Two fingers held up meaning "Victory" or, more likely, how many balls you lost in the water.

WALLET: The thing you have to completely empty out for the privilege of driving yourself crazy in a pastoral setting.

GREENS FEES

WATER HAZARD: Playing 18 holes
after drinking too much soda.

WHIFF: 1) A swing that misses the ball. 2) What you don't want to get, in a compact car, on the way home with your foursome on a 100° day.

"WHOA": What you exclaim on the green as you bat your ball back and forth past the cup. Usually spoken in succession, as in "Whoa! Whoa! Whoa!"

WINTER RULES: Moving the ball for a better lie due to adverse conditions in winter. When applying this rule, remember that it's always winter somewhere.

WOODS: 1) Golf clubs designed to hit the ball a long distance.
2) The place your ball usually lands after being hit a long distance.

X-RAY: What you'll require several of after laughing at your opponent's swing.

YAHOO: Anybody who plays in louder shorts than yours.

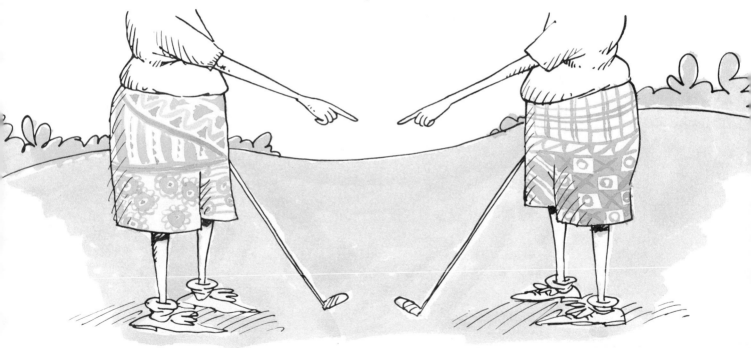

"YOO-HOO": A woman's version of "fore."

ZERO: The number of golfers who could pass a polygraph test.

ZILLION TO ONE: 1) The odds against hitting a hole in one. 2) The odds in favor of hitting a two-inch diameter tree that is 170 yards away.

WRITTEN BY: Chris Brethwaite, Bill Bridgeman, Bill Gray, Allyson Jones, Kevin Kinzer, Mark Oatman, Scott Oppenheimer, Dan Taylor, Rich Warwick and Myra Zirkle.

Books from:

SHOEBOX GREETINGS

(A tiny little division of Hallmark)

STILL MARRIED AFTER ALL THESE YEARS

DON'T WORRY, BE CRABBY: Maxine's Guide to Life

40: THE YEAR OF NAPPING DANGEROUSLY

THE MOM DICTIONARY

THE DAD DICTIONARY

WORKIN' NOON TO FIVE: The Official Workplace Quiz Book

WHAT... ME, 30?

THE FISHING DICTIONARY

YOU EXPECT ME TO SWALLOW THAT? The Official Hospital Quiz Book

THE GOOD, THE PLAID AND THE BOGEY: A Glossary of Golfing Terms

THE CHINA PATTERN SYNDROME: Your Wedding and How to Survive It

THE GRANDPARENT DICTIONARY

STILL A BABE AFTER ALL THESE YEARS?

CRABBY ROAD: More Thoughts on Life From Maxine

THE HANDYMAN DICTIONARY A Guide For the Home Mess-It-Up-Yourselfer